MW01165747

Other Books by the Author

The Death Christ Died: A Case for Unlimited Atonement. A defense of the fact that Christ died for all, not just the elect. Kregel Publishers.

A Biblical Case for Total Inerrancy. A presentation of Christ's view of the inerrancy and authority of Scripture. Kregel Publishers.

The God of the Bible and Other Gods. Presents an outlined introduction to the God presented in Holy Scripture. Kregel Publishers.

Angels, Satan, and Demons. From Satan's debut in Eden, to Christ's victory on Calvary, and into the angelic echelons in Revelation, this book shows what the Bible says about angels, Satan, and demons. Thomas Nelson Publishers.

Safe in the Arms of Jesus. A study of the eternal destiny of infants and others who die before they reach the ability to decide. Kregel Publishers.

The Epistles of First, Second, Third John & Jude. Forgiveness, love, and courage. Kregel Publishers.

Triumph

Through
Tragedy

by

Robert P. Lightner, Th.D.

Associate Professor of Systematic Theology
Dallas Theological Seminary
Dallas, Texas

April 8, 2023

Jo Katie,

*The Lord is good. He spared Bob's
life to serve him over 50 yrs.*

*I thank God for you and your
family. It's His goodness to bring
our 2 families together.*

Love in Christ,

*Pearl Lightner + Bob in heaven
August 3, 2018*

Wipf & Stock
PUBLISHERS
Eugene, Oregon

Dedicated to

Natalie Sue, our baby,
who brought special joy
and comfort to our
family during the days
of trial.

Wipf and Stock Publishers
199 W 8th Ave, Suite 3
Eugene, OR 97401

Triumph Through Tragedy
By Lightner, Robert P.
Copyright©1969 by Lightner, Robert P.
ISBN: 1-59244-995-6
Publication date 11/9/2004
Previously published by Bible Memory Association, Int. , 1969

ACKNOWLEDGEMENTS

A big thank you to Nadine, our middle daughter, who did the cover design.

Grateful recognition is here given also to all who assisted me by supplying information concerning many aspects of the tragedy of which I was unaware because of the nature of my injuries.

In Memoriam

Dr. Carroll Little

Gave his life October 6, 1968 while serving the Lord by assisting those who were trying to advance His cause.

Table of Contents

Chapter   **Page**

Preface 6

Chapter 1 Plans and Preparation 7

Chapter 2 A Mission of Mercy 12

Chapter 3 Fasten Your Seat Belts 17

Chapter 4 Tumble of the Tri-Pacer 20

Chapter 5 Pearl's Diary 26

Chapter 6 A Miracle of Grace 50

Chapter 7 Comfort for Suffering Saints 60

Appendix 68

PREFACE TO THIRD PRINTING

October 6, 1968 seems so long ago now. But I have not forgotten God's marvelous grace in sparing my life that day. I said in the Preface to the First Edition that the important question to ask when tragedy strikes is "Whom am I trusting and in whom is my confidence?"

I still believe that, but over the years since the accident I have been reminded of another important question to ask in times of trouble and trial. "God, what do you want me to learn from this experience?" should be a prime concern. It is not wrong to ask God "why," but we may never get an answer. The "what" question with the attitude of wanting to grow, to mature, is much more important and pleasing to God than the "why" question.

The trials and tragedies of life can make us either bitter or better, and we have to decide which it will be. Our response determines the outcome. I don't ever remember being bitter because of the tragedy. God spared me from that. I do believe He has drawn me closer to Himself and made me more thankful for my family and the privilege of serving Him.

I am the only one still living of those in the plane that crashed. Dr. Little, the pilot, was killed instantly. Dr. and Mrs. Robert Homes divorced some time after the crash. Since then, both have gone to be with the Lord. By God's grace I am still alive and active in His service.

My thanks to Pam Sisson from the Middletown Bible Church in Middletown, Connecticut, who first expressed interest in this project. The two printings made years ago were distributed long ago, and many told me how blessed they were from reading the account. I rejoice in that.

It is my prayer that many more will now be able to also be helped in the journey of life.

Robert Lightner
324 Clear Springs Dr.
Mesquite, TX 75150
972-613-0159
November, 2004

1

PLANS and PREPARATION

"I think I'll learn to fly." My wife, Pearl, heard words like these from me many times. From the time I was about eighteen years old I wanted to learn to fly. My very first time in the air was in the state of Wisconsin in a small Piper-cub with Russell Atkins, a high school buddy of mine. Just after we were airborne, the engine began to miss and run unevenly. Talk about being scared! The pilot, the Reverend Gilbert Howe, discovered very quickly that the gas line had not been opened. Fortunately, he turned some valve, or did something, just in time and the engine kept running and all went well. To use the word *fortunately* is to put the matter mildly because the plane did not have an automatic starter. The pilot had turned the propeller by hand to start the engine. To do that would require rather long legs when you are 1000 feet in the air.

For some reason "first" things stand out in my mind with unusual significance. There are some things in my life I will never forget. That first plane ride is one of them. The most important of them all though is when at age fifteen I was under the conviction of the Holy Spirit to receive Jesus Christ as my personal Saviour. It was a Sunday evening service at what was then called the Lebanon Gospel Center located on the second floor of a dingy building at Seventh and Willow Streets in Lebanon, Pennsylvania. This was denominationally unaffiliated and was hardly even an organized church.

7

As was customary, a Gospel invitation was being given at the close of the service. I felt the need to go to the "altar of prayer," as they called it. "If they sing one more stanza of the hymn I will go," I promised the Lord as I became more and more convicted. To my surprise the leader announced that one more stanza would be sung. I lived up to my promise to the Lord and made my way out of the far end of my row of seats and down the long aisle to the altar and knelt there to be saved.

I knew very little about exactly how to be saved. Several Christians knelt there with me. Some told me to pray more; others told me to believe more. I was confused. One thing was made very clear to me that night by the Spirit of God—I was a sinner in need of Christ as my Saviour. The fact that I was reared in a Christian home did not lessen that inner conviction. I felt like the worst sinner in the world. We had Bible reading and prayer regularly in our home and we rarely missed Sunday school and church. Apart from telling the usual few "white" lies, trying to learn to smoke, and doing what most young growing boys do my life was pretty good, I thought. And I suppose by human standards it was. But it was not human compulsion that brought me to my knees. What more did I need than I already had? Nobody is altogether perfect, you know. It was made crystal clear to me, by an inner voice I could almost hear, that I needed to place my faith in the Lord Jesus Christ as my own personal Saviour from sin.

There at the altar, unfortunately, no one explained to me from the Bible what I needed to do to be saved. I did not know what God expected of me. In spite of this as I knelt there in prayer, truly desirous to be saved and trusting Christ as my personal Saviour as best I knew how, suddenly the burden of sin rolled away and I felt like a new person—I was born again.

Not long after being saved I felt the need to prepare myself for some phase of the Lord's work. After prayer and the counsel of the Reverend George Atkins, now pastor of the Jonestown Bible Church in Jonestown, Pennsylvania, I applied for admission to Baptist Bible Seminary, a Bible College in Johnson City, New York. What an unforgettable "first" that was for me. I knew no one at the school, left Pearl, my steady girl, knew nothing about college life, and suddenly found myself grossly involved in a whole new experience. I thoroughly enjoyed it.

The first weekend I went home was not too enjoyable though. When I was about twenty miles from home and while no doubt daydreaming about seeing my girl friend again, I was involved in a serious auto accident. After being forced off the highway my old Plymouth rolled over several times and landed on its side. Fortunately, I escaped serious injury. Unfortunately, I had to hitchhike home weekends for awhile after that to see Pearl and the folks, and in that order.

There at Bible College I received an education that was truly Christian. During those student days God called me to teach and preach. Without a vision or a dream to confirm it I knew what God wanted me to do. Many experiences in practical Christian work were spiritually rewarding and of lifelong value to me. During those college days after Pearl and I married, First Baptist of Johnson City, N.Y., became our church home and through the years which followed we profited much from its Biblical teaching and the warm fellowship of its people.

My first sermon—what a "first" that was! I will never forget it (and those who heard it probably won't either). In a small country church in the coal regions of Pennsylvania I preached on the question of Job: "How should man be just with God?" (Job 9:2). The people were very patient and kind to put up with my stumbling through that "sermon." From that time on as a student and later as a faculty member at my college alma mater I preached many times. If it had not been for preaching opportunities it would have been very difficult for me to stay in the classroom.

Surprisingly enough, that first plane ride in Wisconsin did not dull my interest in small craft. Several times afterwards I talked seriously with responsible people from Lebanon, Pennsylvania; Johnson City, New York; and Dallas, Texas about the possibility of learning to pilot a small craft. Pearl's lack of enthusiasm for the idea bothered me, but I thought with the right kind of approach and tactics I would sooner or later excite her also. The idea of flying was so strong in my mind that on one occasion I even got some price quotations with the thought of possibly joining with several others in a plane club or owning my own plane sometime in the future. After I heard what it would cost, the idea was quickly dismissed. But the advantages of flying kept haunting me. Just think how much travel time could be saved by flying to a Sunday speaking engagement instead of driving the car. More people could be reached too by having more meetings in more distant places if travel time could be cut.

Through friends, education, and various circumstances over a period of thirty-seven years God was bringing me and preparing me for a tragedy through which He wanted me to triumph. How wise of the sovereign God not to let me know in advance. It is a blessing not to know what tragedies may befall us tomorrow.

In the course of the year in which the tragic plane crash occurred God had led me and my family to Dallas, Texas in mysterious ways. About the same time that the invitation to join the faculty of Dallas Theological Seminary came, other doors of service were opened. At least four other invitations were extended to me to serve the Lord in most exciting places and under challenging, inviting circumstances. My wife and I prayed much for God's will in our decision. I was not seeking a new place of employment. God had blessed and used us at Baptist Bible Seminary. Now He was opening a new door of service for us.

From the human perspective there are a lot of *if's* which come to mind. *If* I had accepted one of the other offers, we would not have been in the State of Texas. *If* we had not been there, I most likely would not have been preaching in Borger, Texas. *If* I had not been willing to run an errand for the Fellowship of Baptists for Home Missions, I would not have been in a plane headed for Hereford, Texas. But how wonderful that there are no *if's* with God and we have also put them aside. We believe we were where God wanted us to be. The decision to come to Dallas was not an easy one nor was it a hurried one. It was made after much agonizing in prayer and only after God had given the signals.

God expects His own to make plans and preparations. This is not a sin. It is a sin though to leave God out of those plans and preparations. The reminder of the Apostle James that this life is like a "vapour, that appeareth for a little time, and then vanisheth away" (James 4:14) is all too easily forgotten. In light of this, all our thoughts, talk, and plans should be captioned with: "If the Lord will, we shall live, and do this, or that" (James 4:15).

2

A MISSION of MERCY

Of all the possibilities of taking flying instruction the best and most likely seemed to be when we moved from Johnson City, New York to Dallas, Texas. After the decision was made to join the faculty of Dallas Theological Seminary we soon found ourselves living in Dallas. No, the Seminary does not offer flight instruction, but we did purchase a home about one half mile from a very active small-craft landing strip and a flight instruction school, the White Rock Airport. This could very well have rekindled my interest in learning to fly.

For two of our girls, coming to Dallas was returning to the place of their birth. Nancy Kay was born in Baylor University Hospital, February 7, 1959 during my student days at Dallas Seminary. Nadine Pearl was born June 5, 1962 in the same hospital when I was doing my graduate study at Dallas Seminary while on leave of absence from the faculty of Baptist Bible Seminary. Our third girl, Natalie Sue, was born July 16, 1968 in Lourdes Hospital, Binghamton, New York and was just five weeks old when we moved to Dallas in August.

However, before the thought of learning to fly could be entertained, an opportunity to preach came along.

Dr. J. Elwood Evans, Dean of Students of Dallas Theological Seminary, asked whether I would be interested in preaching in a place called Borger, Texas. Dr. Evans was responsible for supplying preachers for a group there. I had never heard of the place. It turned out that Borger was a town of 18 to 20,000 people where a sizeable group of believers became dissatisfied with the ministry, emphasis, and liberal affiliation of their church and decided to start an independent work. What a challenge that presented to me and with little hesitation I said, "Yes, I'll go to preach."

Borger is located about fifty miles northwest of Amarillo, Texas which is approximately 450 miles west of Dallas. That would mean a long hard drive. The flight schedule from Dallas Love Field Airport to Amarillo was most convenient though. Reservations were made for flight on Braniff International Airways. One of the gentlemen from the Borger group was to meet me at the Amarillo airport and take me to the place of meeting. That gentleman was Mr. Paul Husen. We had good fellowship as we motored to Borger that day.

My first visit there on the Sunday of September 15 proved to be most enjoyable. The message from God's Word in Isaiah 6:1-8 on the holiness of God was received with real warmth and enthusiasm by a group of about one hundred people. Isaiah lived in a spiritually dark day, a day like ours. He needed to be reminded of the awesome authority of God. When God, through a vision, made him aware of that, then Isaiah saw the awfulness of his own sin, even though he was a prophet of God. When God's holiness and his own sin were recognized, Isaiah then became aware of his own responsibility before God and said, "Here am I; send me."

The service that Sunday was held in a building owned by the Phillips 66 Company. Borger is an oil town and the Phillips 66 Company employs many people since it has a large refinery there. After the noon meal at the home of Mr. & Mrs. Husen, my host and hostess for the day, there was a short meeting with representatives of the group. Ideas and suggestions concerning the possibilities and the future of the group were discussed. Memories of past days in Johnson City, New York when I was associated with Baptist Bible Seminary and engaged in rather extensive weekend ministries came to mind. The group in Borger seemed just as enthusiastic and eager to go on for God as several other groups with which I had been privileged to work.

The following week a letter came to me from Dr. Kenneth Muck, who was the General Director of the Fellowship of Baptists for Home Missions. Dr. Muck's burden concerned the possibility of opening a new independent Baptist work in Hereford, Texas. Since I was located in Dallas, Dr. Muck wondered whether I could visit Hereford and search out the possibilities of a church being organized there. In fact, a church building was available to the Mission for this purpose.

It seemed logical that this survey should be made on my next visit to Borger since Borger is just about one hundred miles from Hereford. Plans were formulated for another preaching ministry to Borger for October 6. Through a phone conversation I arranged to meet the gentleman in Hereford on Sunday afternoon who was to assist me by showing me the building and answering my questions. After investigating the flight schedule and cost of flying from Borger to Hereford, I decided rather to attempt to use a car owned by someone in the Borger group or to ask them to drive me to Hereford. However, upon learning that Dr. Carroll Little, a local dentist and one of the men in the group for whom I was preaching, needed just a few more hours of flying time before receiving his pilot's license and that he was going to fly anyway, I agreed to let him fly me to Hereford.

The message to the group that morning was titled "The Great Divider." The text was John 9. Christ was and is the great divider of men. That sounds strange in this ecumenical age. But wherever He went, whatever He said or did brought division among the people. "There was a division among the people because of him" (John 7:43). Then and now some respond to the claims of Christ with a believing heart as did the blind man. Many others, as did the Pharisees, respond with an unbelieving heart. Still others attempt to do what the parents of the blind man sought to do—remain uncommitted to Christ. This was, and still is, impossible to do. Either a man is for Christ or against Him; one of the choices is inevitable. To make either one is to eliminate the other. Neutral you cannot be in relation to Christ.

After the morning service several of us went to the cafeteria located in the lower floor of the Borger Hotel where they were renting a large room and other facilities for the church services at that time. We then agreed to go to the home of Dr. and Mrs. Robert L. Holmes where a short meeting was held to consider a name for the anticipated church, and we also planned our trip to Hereford.

It was from this meeting that we departed for the airport to board the Tri-Pacer N2642A. Dr. Holmes, a practicing physician in Borger, and his wife, Bille Holmes, both licensed pilots with a lot of flying experience and also members of the group, agreed to go along on the mission of mercy to Hereford.

The Ohio National Guard, the State Highway Patrol and the University Hospital have formed a team using "medicopters" to rush physicians, medical equipment, and medicines directly to scenes of accidents. After professional emergency treatment is rendered, the injured persons are transported to the University Hospital in the helicopter for further treatment. Tom Thomson, writing for *Minutes*, the magazine for a large insurance company, called the helicopters used for this service "Whirlybirds of Mercy."

While we were not going in a helicopter or trying to rescue someone involved in a crash, we were nevertheless all bound on a mission of mercy. In one way or another, each of us was attempting to perform a ministry for the Lord.

15

HUTCHINSON COUNTY AIRPORT BORGER, TEXAS			FLIGHT PLAN

FLIGHT PLAN

HUTCHINSON COUNTY AIRPORT
BORGER, TEXAS

1. TYPE OF FLIGHT PLAN	2. AIRCRAFT IDENTIFICATION	3. AIRCRAFT TYPE	4. TRUE AIRSPEED	5. DEPARTURE TIME
☒ VFR ☐ DVFR ☐ IFR	N-2642A	Tripacer PA 22	118 KNOTS	PROPOSED (Z) 2135 ACTUAL (Z)

6. INITIAL CRUISING ALTITUDE	7. POINT OF DEPARTURE	8. ROUTE OF FLIGHT
6500	Borger	direct

9. DESTINATION (Name of airport and city)	10. ESTIMATED TIME EN ROUTE		11. FUEL ON BOARD		12. ALTERNATE AIRPORT(S)
	HOURS	MINUTES	HOURS	MINUTES	
Hereford		45	4	00	

13. REMARKS

14. PILOT'S NAME	15. PILOT'S ADDRESS OR AIRCRAFT HOME BASE	16. NO. OF PERSONS ABOARD
Carroll G. Little	317 Garrett Borger, Texas	4

17. COLOR OF AIRCRAFT	18. FLIGHT WATCH
tan & white	

CLOSE FLIGHT PLAN UPON ARRIVAL

SEE REVERSE

A flight plan like the above was filed by Carroll Little at the Borger airport before we took off.

16

3

FASTEN YOUR SEAT BELTS

After a short meeting at the Holmes' residence that lovely afternoon of October 6, 1968 we made our way to the local airport to fly to Hereford. Dr. and Mrs. Holmes and I traveled together to the Borger Hutchinson County Airport, which had a crash free record since it opened in 1949. Dr. Little, who was to pilot the craft, left the Holmes' residence before we did to preflight check the plane. Kiddingly, I said to Dr. Little as he left for the airport, "Be sure to take my briefcase with you and put it in the plane because I have my insurance policy in it." The preflight checkout indicated everything was normal and the plane was ready to go. The flight plan, filed before takeoff at the airport, indicated the small craft was bound for Hereford (where I was scheduled to investigate the possibilities of starting the mission church). We were scheduled to land at the Hereford Municipal Airport.

How exciting to think of flying with such distinguished people! After all, it isn't every day in the week that a preacher is in the company of professional people who love and want to serve Jesus Christ. When traveling on commercial airlines I often thought how thrilling it would be to be close enough to the pilot so that I could see him in operation and watch all the gauges, switches, and controls. Now at long last, at least in a small craft, I was going to be able to do just that. The plane we boarded was owned by Dr. Little and two other doctors who were in the process of forming a flying club. Mechanically, it was in top-notch condition.

Dr. Carroll Little was a successful dentist in the city. He graduated from Texas A & M University and also the University of Texas Dental School in 1962. He was born March 24, 1930 at Goldsboro, Texas and had been a resident of Borger since July, 1962 when he moved from Houston, Texas. Since moving to Borger he had been a member of the First Presbyterian Church there. Also, he was a member of the Panhandle District Dental Society and the North Plains Knife and Fork Club. As a First Lieutenant in the Army he was a veteran of the Korean War. His student pilot's license was indicative of considerable hours of flying time behind him. Before taking his flying test for a pilot's license he needed a cross country flight. This trip to Hereford would provide that.

Beside Dr. Little was Mrs. Holmes, acting as copilot. Behind Dr. Little I was seated and beside me was Dr. Holmes, the second licensed pilot aboard. Mrs. Bille Holmes had participated, just three months before, in the twenty-second annual Powder Puff Derby as the copilot of a plane flown by a woman from Odessa. The two women placed thirty-fourth in the Derby.

I was the only one in the plane without any flying experience. I was in good hands and no one had any reason for fear. After final checks were all made on the plane and all seat belts were fastened, we headed down runway number 210. The takeoff was very ordinary and everything was quite normal. In a short time we were about 500 feet in the air. Dr. Holmes thought he sensed that Dr. Little was having some difficulty. The plane seemed to be hard to handle. The men chatted briefly about it but they were not overly concerned. The problem related to the plane's trim tab and was not a serious difficulty. The trim tab is a means of assisting the pilot to keep the plane level and assists in controlling the direction of the nose and tail of the craft. The trim tab is really a convenience for the pilot.

18

He does not need to work as hard at keeping the plane on a straight and level course when the trim tab is functioning properly. However, it is possible to fly a small craft, such as we were in, even without the use of the trim tab. To do so, however, would be like driving a car with one front tire about half flat. Dr. Holmes suggested that Dr. Little change the control and see if there would be any improvement. Dr. Little did this, but there was no change. Then Dr. Holmes said rather than work so hard to fly the plane all the way to Hereford, we should return to the Borger airport and check the trim tab to be sure it was functioning properly and that the control was being moved properly.

We landed without any difficulty and taxied to a convenient spot. Dr. Little went outside and made sure the trim tab was responding to the control in the cockpit. It was, and there did not appear to be any malfunction. Before the plane was moved again, Dr. Holmes offered the use of his own twin engine six-passenger Astec which was already gassed up. Dr. Little said all was well and there was no need to use the other plane. After being on the ground about five minutes, we headed down runway number 170 for our second takeoff. A T-28 World War II trainer plane was ahead of us on the same runway. After the T-28 was airborne, we took off. All was going well until . . .

4

TUMBLE of the TRI-PACER

We had just gotten off the ground and were 150 or 200 feet in the air when all aboard sensed that the plane simply refused to climb any higher. We were traveling 80 or 90 miles per hour at the south end of the runway on a straight course. The plane began to lose altitude. Suddenly trees and houses appeared ahead of us. To avoid hitting them Dr. Little began a shallow left turn. As he did so, he found himself heading toward the huge KHUZ local radio tower. The left turn was then steepened to avoid the tower. When this was done, the plane stalled out and crashed. We hit on the edge of a local country macadam road. The gouges where the plane first hit and the propeller tore up the asphalt were visible for a long time afterward. The engine was torn completely from the plane and the pieces finally settled just off the edge of the road and on the edge of an embankment.

Our plane crashed hitting first on the left wing and then on the nose. Before coming to a stop the small plane cartwheeled about 250 feet. When it finally stopped, it was no longer a plane or hardly even recognizable as one. Somewhere inside that twisted heap of steel, with gasoline soaked all over it and its passengers, were three human beings who had been on a mission of mercy.

Dr. Little, the fourth one on a mission of mercy, was thrown from the plane. He lay along the road, after the plane had rolled over him, flat on his stomach in a

This is an actual photo of the crashed plane. Three human beings were jammed inside this twisted wreckage.

stretched out position. His seat belt had torn loose from the plane's chassis. Mrs. Holmes was hanging partly out of the wreckage. Dr. Holmes was slumped deep down in his seat. Both of the Holmes' still had their seat belts on. My seat belt was still secured also though I was almost thrown from the plane. I was partly in and partly out of the wreckage. Dr. Holmes was the only one conscious through the entire ordeal. He lifted the upholstered ceiling of the plane, which had fallen all over me, and saw my battered and bloody face and heard me breathing. The first thing Dr. Holmes did, of course, was to scream for help. He wouldn't have needed to, however, because help was on its way.

Mr. Mather E. Griffin, manager of the Hutchinson County Airport, flight instructor, and close friend of Dr. Little, discovered we were having difficulty, saw our plane descending to the ground and obviously out of control, and rushed with Mr. Martin Glaze and Mr. A. E. Nix to the wrecked craft. As the men sped to the site of the crash, about one quarter mile from the airport, Mr. Griffin did a very wise thing. He warned the men of the danger involved in trying to rescue people from a wreckage. Later, a word of warning was also given to those who had gathered to observe. Sometimes there is more harm done during attempted rescue than was done in the accident itself.

When these men arrived at the crash, what they found was terrible to behold! Their job was to rescue the perishing. They did a most commendable job. Dr. Holmes spoke to Mr. Griffin as soon as he arrived, only minutes after the tumble of the Tri-Pacer. He asked if his wife was alive and the reply was "yes." Dr. Holmes reminded Mr. Griffin that gasoline was dripping down over him. When Mr. Griffin tried to get Mrs. Holmes out of the plane, he found it impossible. Her slacks had caught on a piece of metal which made her rescue difficult. The rescuers thought that she possibly had a broken neck and back. Dr. Holmes assisted Mr. Griffin by freeing her, and they finally got her out. It was feared that Dr. Little was probably not alive since he had been thrown from the plane. Dr. Holmes asked for two men to help him up out of the seat where he was jammed. After taking a few steps he realized that something was seriously wrong with his back and chest. He had the men lay him down to wait for the second ambulance. Dr. Holmes thinks I regained consciousness long enough to help them get me out. Even after the rescuers put me on an ambulance cart, I got up and walked around in a daze. After I was laid down again, an alert Mr. Griffin heard me gurgling and having difficulty breathing and quickly had my head placed in a position so the excessive bleeding would not cause me to choke.

Mrs. Holmes and I were taken in to the North Plains Hospital in Borger on the first ambulance and only minutes later Drs. Little and Holmes on the second one to the same hospital. The plane wreckage was carefully guarded by the Borger Civil Air Patrol for some time. The area was roped off pending the arrival of the Federal Aviation Administration officials from Lubbock and Oklahoma City.

After a very brief stay in the Borger hospital I was taken to the Northwest Texas Hospital in Amarillo about fifty miles away. After my X-rays were developed, Dr. Wheeler promptly ordered me taken there because of the nature of my injuries. Before we had arrived at the hospital, Dr. Holmes had asked that his associates, Drs. Knowles and Wheeler, and his personal friend, Dr. Prewitt, who was also associated with the church group, be contacted and be standing by at the hospital. After the X-rays on the Holmes' were developed and Dr. Little had been pronounced dead by Drs. Wheeler and Knowles, Dr. Holmes was sent via the second ambulance to the Amarillo hospital also. Mrs. Holmes stayed in the Borger hosptial until the next day when she was then moved to Amarillo.

Dr. Little was a believer in Jesus Christ as his Saviour, a devoted husband and father, and a strong supporter of the Borger church group. He was thirty-eight years old. He is survived by his wife, Jimmie; a son, Grant, six years old; and two daughters, Jaycile, eighteen years old, and Susan, eight years old.

Enroute to Amarillo the driver of the second ambulance was going about 110 miles per hour. That is fast even on a straight Texas highway! Dr. Holmes told him to slow down because they were not in that big a hurry and the swaying of the ambulance was hurting his back and pelvis. The driver then slowed to 80 or 90 miles per hour.

It is only natural to ask, "What caused the Tri-Pacer to crash?" Perhaps we will never know for sure. Probably, a combination of circumstances caused it. The major and most likely reason for the tumble of the Tri-Pacer has been described as "wake turbulence." In the November, 1968 issue of *Flying*, an aviation magazine, an article with that caption appears. Dr. Holmes feels certain that this is what caused the crash. I respect his evaluation and judgment very much since he was in the plane, witnessed the entire crash, and is an experienced pilot himself.

Archie Trammell, the associate editor of *Flying*, calls "wake turbulence" potentially aviation's "biggest killer." Some pilots refer to this problem as "prop wash." Others assume this is only a problem where there are large jets, and some feel the problem has been exaggerated. Trammell says all three attitudes are wrong. He and others have experimented chasing jets and other aircraft in an especially designed craft to discover the facts concerning "wake turbulence." He defines and explains it this way: "What causes it? An airplane, you recall, planes along on a cushion of air. Thus there is a differential pressure between the top and bottom of the plane. The higher air pressure below has a passion to neutralize the lower pressure on top. Since it cannot go around the front or back of the wing because of its momentum, it flows laterally along the span and slips up and around the tip. This current up around the tip is what generates the wing-tip vortex. Tests have shown that the heavier the airplane, the greater the turbulence. If this is true, then as the angle of the attack is increased, the pressure differential will increase and thus increase the turbulence."

Trammell makes another observation which throws light upon the tumble of the Tri-Pacer. Remember we took off the second time after a T-28 trainer had used the same runway and had become airborne. "Make no mistake: the greatest action comes in the takeoff and final approach phases of flight, just when the ground is nearest." Those who have studied this problem insist there are times when there is no way to predict where the greatest danger will be. The Federal Aviation Administration has a movie and pamphlet on "wake turbulence," and even they do not try to provide all the answers.

The question remains, "What can be done, if after all possible precaution, a pilot still hits a wake or the vortex created by another plane?" Trammell's answer to this question is exactly what Dr. Little attempted to do even though he may not have been aware that he was in a "wake turbulence": "We found that we could get out of them the quickest in the Citabria by going to full power and starting a turn. The vorticies are really quite small in cross-section, and the farther from the core you are, the less the velocity of the roll. So, hit the power, turn out and go around."

In spite of all that Dr. Little tried to do and in spite of the fine craftsmanship of the plane, the Tri-Pacer still tumbled. If that radio tower had not been in our way, he might have been successful in coming out of the wake. The tragic tumble was fatal to one and near fatal to three.

5

PEARL'S DIARY

The following represents selections from the meticulous diary which my wife, Pearl, kept from October 6, the day of the crash, to October 23, when I was released from Presbyterian Hospital in Dallas. These portions of her treasured account covering those days are being reproduced here as she wrote it day by day, with only minor changes.

Sunday, October 6, 1968

Bob left 7:00 a.m. to fly to Amarillo to preach at Borger.

6:30 p.m.—Dr. Rex Prewitt called from Borger. Said Bob was in plane crash at 4:30. Pilot killed! Bob taken to Amarillo with facial injuries, probably needs plastic surgery. Dr. and Mrs. Holmes were badly hurt.

I called Northwest Texas Hospital in Amarillo and located a Dr. Hands, surgeon. He had stitched Bob's lip which was cut up to and into the nose and was lying open. They did a tracheotomy for breathing. Face was mashed and later swelling was terrific. He has compound skull fracture and is bleeding from the ear. The bleeding and swelling of the brain could kill him anytime; the first 48 hours are the most critical! I'm numb. Couldn't call friends right away as I knew they'd be in church.

Two neighbor men went to Love Field, located the car and brought it home.

26

Five neighbor ladies stayed until Drs. Hendricks,* Getz,* and Campbell* came to the house. Called Dr. Hands of the Amarillo hospital at 10:00 p.m. Four or five doctors are on the case and Bob is still unconscious.

Elaine Getz* spent the night with me. Girls and I cried a lot, afraid their Daddy will die. Both girls said, "He'll never laugh again and he won't think right," when I told them he's unconscious and has compound skull fracture.

I kept "hoping" I was in a dream, or there was a mistake somewhere and soon he would arrive home and walk in the door. All night I planned the funeral that might be necessary, where I'd live, what I'd do, etc. and I prayed and cried. Slept 2½ hours.

Monday, October 7

Dr. Kenneth Johnston** and Marie Keeler** both called from Amarillo. They had seen Bob and he nodded and responded. The Johnstons (Ken and Mary Bell**) had moved to Amarillo from Oklahoma City in June. We didn't know this. He said I could stay with them if and when I come and Mary Bell will help with the baby if I bring her. This is a miracle. The Lord went before me in this. What else could I do? Where would I stay with Natalie? Called my mother and asked her to fly down from Pennsylvania. Dr. Ryrie* got her at 8:00 p.m.

Mrs. Walvoord came in the morning. Dr. Walvoord* called me from Illinois. Nadine stayed home from school—cried quite a bit. Nancy took courage and went to school. The Lord is helping them.

Elaine stayed till noon. Then Ann Ryrie* came till evening. She brought supper.

*Dallas Seminary faculty members and their wives will be noted in this way throughout the diary.

**Friends from student days will be indicated this way throughout.

I decided to keep nursing Natalie as long as I can. So far she is O.K. Dr. Jordan, my doctor, said to keep nursing. Dr. Hands of Amarillo reported that Bob spoke a few words. He said it was a miracle that he was able to talk and respond with all his injuries. He couldn't understand it. It was decided I would not go to Amarillo yet. I have the girls to arrange for and consider. If Bob were conscious and could advise me, I know he'd have much concern that I care for the girls. Dr. Hands said he'd let us know as soon as Bob begins getting conscious or if he should turn worse and when he recommends I come since at this time he still wouldn't know me. To think of seeing him like this scares me!

Karolyn Kempton** called and said when I go to Amarillo to look up her sister for any help. Got a call from First Baptist, Johnson City, N.Y., telling that they are having round the clock prayer. Talked to his brother Harold and Gleason Ritchie**—Jonestown Bible Church is praying. Harold said his mother blames herself as she didn't have time to pray for her children that morning as she usually does.

We're all so jumpy when phone rings—fear bad news.

Tuesday, October 8

We get telegrams and phone calls from different parts of the country from long time friends assuring me of love and prayers. Dallas Seminary is having special prayer groups and also Baptist Bible Seminary in Clarks Summit, Pa.

It's good to have Mother—answer to prayer that she could get off work and come so soon to stay with the girls. I even went to PTA at night to hear Nadine sing with her first grade class. The neighbors have been wonderful.

Dr. Hendricks made plane reservations for me to fly to Amarillo tomorrow. He had offered to drive me over if I wanted to go that way, but I knew flying would be easier and quicker for Natalie and me.

Mrs. Walvoord brought in a meal. All are so wonderful to us.

I'm learning lessons. Feel arms of Lord under me. Sunday night, all during the night, I felt so helpless so I looked up 1 Peter 5:7, "He careth for you" and then saw verse 6, "Humble yourselves therefore under the mighty hand of God." Monday morning I found Psalm 73:26, "My flesh and my heart faileth: but God is the strength of my heart." The only thing I can do is cling to these verses. This is all strange for me—I've never had anything like this before.

Dr. Prewitt called saying he had picked up Bob's things—wallet, etc. I cried when he told of Dr. Little's family, ages 6, 8 and 18.

Wednesday, October 9

Thunderstorms and dark outside.

Dr. Little's funeral today.

Flew with Natalie to Amarillo. The unknown weighs heavily—don't know how long I'll have to stay, how long he'll be there, how long Mother can stay, etc. I'm staying with Ken and Mary Bell Johnston (Dr. Johnston).

I saw Bob a few minutes at 4:00 p.m. He's in ICU (Intensive Care Unit). Looks like he has a mask on his face, black all around eyes and cheeks. Others had prepared me that he wouldn't be recognizable but still it was a shock to see him. Swelling is intense and like a balloon. Face moves oddly when he swallows, upper jaw doesn't move at all, he has floating maxilla and loose teeth. He kept saying, "How are my girls, how is my mother? I feel miserable; what happened?" When I'd say, "You were in an accident," he'd say, "Was it a plane crash?" Doctors had told him but he seemed to want my confirmation. He said, "I'm all banged up, I guess I look a mess, I could have been killed. Am I going to be all right?" I said, "Do you know me?" He said, "Oh, sure, you are my wife." He kept saying, "You are precious to me." He'd take his hand and point all around his face and say, "It's all dried up; I feel miserable." He

29

doesn't seem to be aware of his broken wrist and dislocated thumb; it's bandaged and in a splint. I can see the thumb is pushed in; it looks short.

Dr. Hale, ear, nose, and throat surgeon, came in and said they'd be doing surgery the next a.m. to wire teeth and jaw (to be in for 6 weeks), fix maxilla which is all broken and repair the blowout of his right eye. His eyes are swollen, almost closed, and are black and red inside from bleeding. Also, in surgery they'll set broken wrist and fix dislocated thumb which can't be set from the outside. Also, will fix broken nose.

I saw Dr. Holmes who was also in the crash and now was brought back to the Intensive Care Unit (has difficulty breathing) where Bob still is.

At night I saw Bob again and he seemed to say same things. He "dozes" between words. Kept saying, "The nurses and doctors are so sweet to me. They take such good care of you here. Tell my girls to pray. I love them very much. I love my Nanner (Nancy) and Deanie (Nadine)."

Thursday, October 10

Surgery at 9:15 a.m.

I had told the nurse about Bob's previous nasal problem and headaches and asked if she'd see that the doctors get the information before surgery.

11:45—Back in ICU. Surgery finished at 11:30. *Praise God!*

Dan Gelatt** got me on phone in waiting room during surgery.

12:30—Dr. Curtis, oral surgeon, informed me complications can still come. Antibiotics are given to prevent infection which could occur because of opening from skull to outside. He put wires inside Bob's face and connected them to eyebones to hold his jaw and facial bones in place which are broken in many places. Loose teeth are wired in and braces put in. Cheek bone was set under eye by Dr.

30

Hale. Dr. Hyde, orthopedic surgeon, did his wrist and thumb. He might be in ICU a week. It's a miracle they can do so much with such severe injuries—broken bones.

Talked to Mrs. Holmes and found out plane had taken off twice, had landed once to take care of some trivial thing!??? She has concussion, bad cuts all over face, bad chipped heel and broken arm. Dr. Holmes still has pieces of fat in his blood stream which is dangerous.

Pat (Keeler) Dewey,** Marie's older daughter, kept Natalie; I used her car. Could hardly find my way back to her house but felt the Lord's guidance.

Saw Dr. Hands. He explained medicine was given Sunday night to shrink brain to make room for bleeding. He also explained how when Bob was brought to emergency the nurses couldn't get a doctor at first so they called him and he came to the hospital and stitched him up as Bob was vomiting blood which could get in his lungs which would be serious. He said nurses thought he was serious and needed help. He did!! He explained the blowout of the right eye would cause a crossed eye if not pushed back in place. Face was elongated and one side pushed over at eye. Dr. Hands told me he is staying on the case to watch over him in an overall capacity as each of the other surgeons watches a particular thing and something else could develop in the rest of the body and go unnoticed. He said, "Sometimes a patient is lost in this way!"

I met more of the Borger people. I'm impressed that they are so sincere and deeply concerned and so sorry this happened. They told me Mrs. Little is holding up but is so puzzled why it happened and feels responsible.

All of this discussion of details of the crash and then to see Bob in pain and suffering is exhausting me. I am physically and mentally exhausted.

Friday, October 11

Barbara (Keeler) Hedger,** Marie's younger daughter, took me to hospital and kept Natalie.

31

I called Kathryn White, Karolyn Kempton's twin sister.

Bob was able to talk better but not able to move his face except bottom lip. Swelling and blackness is starting to decrease. Starting to get yellow so it will heal, it seems.

12:00 p.m.—I was able to give him liquid through a straw. Tracheotomy and intravenous tubes are gone.

3:00 p.m.—He talked more, asked if I was on the plane, where he was going and if it was after a service. He asked about the girls and named all three. Before, he'd only mention Nancy and Nadine. It seems more recent events are coming back in his memory.

I talked to Dr. Holmes. He said they all feel so badly that this happened to my husband. He said when they had crashed and were sitting on the ground and no one said a word, he thought, "My God, what have we done." He is now out of ICU.

Bob is suffering but he is so brave. One of the nurses said, "It's a pleasure to care for him."

Mrs. Little's mother and sister came to meet me and said Mrs. Little is doing fine but goes off and weeps and is so concerned for me.

4:30 p.m.—Marie Keeler came to get Natalie and me and we moved to her house, baby bed and all, for the weekend as Johnstons are going to Dallas. They are letting me use their car.

Bob told me he screamed when they took out his stitches (this must have been in yesterday's surgery).

I called Mother in Dallas. Talked to Nancy and Nadine. They ask so many questions—ones hard for me to answer about Bob.

10:00 p.m.—Bob asked if anyone was killed on the plane.

I'M SO TIRED! Each day arrangements and plans must be made for the care of Natalie and plans must be worked around her schedule of feedings and naps. Too, driving strange cars from various homes to hospital in strange place is tiring. I try to get to the hospital three times each day, traveling back and forth to nurse and feed the baby. Each time I stay there for a few hours so I can visit more than once. Sometimes I miss the 2 hour interval of the 5 minute visit of the ICU but nurses have allowed me to go in on off times and let me stay a little longer. The Lord is helping me—I need it!

Saturday, October 12

Today is my birthday.

Bob's swelling is going down, blackness getting more yellow. He asks where he was and where he was going. Nurses in ICU told me to be honest in my answers to him. He just says, "Oh," when I answer or explain. He asked, "I wonder how long I'll be here." He wouldn't take much fluid today, says he's stuffed.

I was so exhausted so didn't get back in the afternoon till 5:00 and was so shocked as they had moved him from ICU to second floor. No one seemed to be watching him like in ICU. I tried to give him supper but he can't open his mouth and it's hard to get anything in. With jaws clamped tightly shut, and nose packing in, it's hard to breathe, much less to swallow. I tried it myself. No wonder he takes very little liquid. He sips it through his lips and teeth. And also, he's moaning for pain now.

Saw Dr. Hyde and he said they must do more fixing on the wrist on Tuesday and by the end of next week his part is done and Bob could go to Dallas, but the other doctors must give their consent.

Talked to Bob's mother and she and Ken, Bob's brother, and his wife want to fly to Amarillo next weekend. She would then go to Dallas and his brother would fly back to Lebanon.

My mother told me on phone that cards, letters, and phone calls are pouring in to Dallas too. And many are sending gifts of money and also Dallas Seminary students are assisting financially. I haven't even thought of medical bills; it's immaterial up to now. I've not been able to contain or think of so much. Our phone bill will be astronomical too but I feel I must call some people to keep them informed and share my burdens. It is a help to talk to Mother. Since she works in a hospital, her medical knowledge and knowing what to expect in Bob's case and in hospital procedure is a tremendous help.

I picked up Bob's cut up suit and shirt. Didn't look at it though! I came home from hospital quite early, 9:00 p.m., as I can't seem to do much for Bob. He sleeps all the time—is weary from pain. I long to bear some of the pain and suffering for him. I'm so discouraged and confused—don't know what to do next. There are so many details and responsibilities for me alone. If only others were *here* to help with visiting and caring for him and sharing the burden.

Nancy Jacobs** called; she reminded me someone far better than humans is watching over Bob. Ann Ryrie also called. The continued phone calls assuring us of love and prayers do help.

Poured out my heart and fears about Bob's condition to Marie Keeler, bless her heart. She and Mary Bell have been so sweet, seeing that I get good food, caring for baby and willing to bear my outbursts of emotion.

As I was driving home on the expressway at night I found myself singing parts of "The Lord Gave Me A Song." Humanly, I surely can't "sing." The opposite, that of despair for Bob's suffering, is the way I feel. I hardly knew what I was doing. It seemed someone else was singing it. I've never experienced anything like this before. It *must* have been the Lord!

Sunday, October 13

10:00 a.m.—Went to the hospital. Drs. Hands and Curtis came to see Bob when I was there. It will be another week before he can go to Dallas. It's amazing how each doctor watches certain things. If he does not get enough liquids, he will need intravenous again.

Bob talks more. Asked who the pilot was. I said "Dr. Little" and he said "oh." He sat up a few times. Asked "What about my teaching load?" Also asked about the girls. He said his arm hurts (first time he's mentioned this). He asked details of the crash and asked if Dr. Evans* was on the plane (indicates he knows about Borger). He still has bleeding from the ear—danger of infection. They give antibiotics for it. He asked who is taking care of the baby.

Dr. Price, neurosurgeon, came in. He said definitely there was brain damage but he thinks it will recover. He thinks it won't be permanent. He thinks Bob might be able to fly to Dallas hospital by Friday. He said the shock and pain make him sleep, not only the sedation.

3:30 p.m.—He asked me again about his teaching load and asked who was taking his classes. He asked, "What does my Daddy think?" He said, "I don't ever want to go on a plane again." He said, "I'm a nuisance and worthless to the Lord." He doesn't comprehend things when I answer and explain. And he asks same things over again, doesn't remember what I've said or when I've been in.

At noon Kathryn, Karolyn's sister, came and Bob perked right up and said, "I can see she is Karolyn's sister." I cried to see her as it seemed Karolyn was here.

He wouldn't take much liquid at noon.

They check his eyes, blood pressure, etc., every hour.

He has drainage too from the ear—from bones and blood vessels inside.

Dr. Lindsey,* who preached at Borger today, and friends from Borger came. Borger people said they are starting a fund for us to help with expenses! The Lord is going before in this also. Money has been farthest from my mind.

I moved back to Johnstons at night. They had been to see Mother and my girls in Dallas and brought back birthday gifts from them for me and also packs of mail that came to Dallas.

I'm so worried for Bob to be all alone all night. I guess the family is expected to help with the patient but I just can't be there.

Monday, October 14

It's *so sad* as he seems worse in his mind—very incoherent. He said, "It's hopeless." (This isn't like him).

He has a real bad rash. Starting at noon he could have no liquids—they'll work on his arm in the morning.

I cried so much, ache for his suffering.

I almost got lost on way home at night. Guess I'm getting irrational too.

Mrs. Little came to see me and poured out her heart. The plane was total loss and not insured. And also her husband had no liability insurance. People have been asking me about this. She keeps asking "What caused the crash?" "Why?"

Dr. Hale put in tracheotomy again to help his breathing. He's getting intravenous as he can't take any liquid by mouth because of surgery tomorrow. Dr. Hale explained the nose packing could come out soon. He said in 6 weeks Bob might have double vision. The sinus bone, the base, was broken but was intact so they didn't do an implant; it should heal. If it doesn't, his eye may look lower to us and he may have to have an implant put in.

Oh, all this is unbearable! He is so thirsty and dry, just begs for water and keeps asking for damp cloth for his lips (we get it for him quite often). He even asked me to spray his throat. He said, "This is torture; you have no idea."

Mother called in evening and said I should call Dr. Ryrie and we should contact Dr. Mabery, ear, nose, and throat specialist, who will take Bob's case in Dallas. And I should try to contact Dr. Hands so he knows about Dr. Mabery as I had given another doctor's name before.

36

When I got back to Johnstons at night, Ken talked to me and said Bob does have sedation and he's depressed (which is to be expected) which all causes some of the irrationality. But the fact that he reacts to him like he does shows his mind is going to be all right. It helps to have a personal friend who is also a doctor to reassure me and explain things.

But I'm worried about his mind. I know he seems normal when others talk to him. But to me he's not the same. I know bones can heal and scars and looks don't mean everything. But the mind . . . If he can't teach and preach, what will he do? That's his life. I told the Lord I'd be willing to have him taken if his mind won't be normal. I'm concerned that his personality might be affected and he'll be discouraged—not his sunny self; he's always been the one to encourage and brighten the family.

Tuesday, October 15

I'm so tired!

Bob had surgery to have the bones fitted together in a better position in his wrist. They were splintered so they didn't hold or go right the first time. He was back in his room by 11:00.

I called Dr. Jackson** (at that time the National Representative of General Association of Regular Baptist Churches, who is now with the Lord) in Chicago and told him all about it and my burdens.

Dr. Hyde came in and said bones are together real well now. They want to check out his spine before they let him go to Dallas. Dr. Price told me they will X-ray his skull again also.

Dr. Hale took out the packing in his nose in the afternoon and he said Dr. Mabery of Dallas would be fine to have charge of Bob. He said Bob's nose must have been in a thousand pieces and he thinks it is looking pretty good.

37

He hates to keep putting the tracheotomy tube back in so he asked if surgery went all right in the morning.

When Bob got awake from surgery, he seemed like he woke up from a dream. He said, "Patience! I've learned a lot." I said, "What have you learned?" He said, "To trust the Lord." When I left, he said, "Be careful." Also he put his hand on my face for the first time.

When I came back in the afternoon, he seemed so much better—he can breathe. He looked all around (becoming aware of the surroundings). He asked about the family and how I could be there so long and spend so much time. He drank and said, "Tastes like a million. I could cry like a baby; it tastes so good." I gave him a back rub and it felt so good to him. He seems like his loving self—praise God! I know there will still be rough spots and Dr. Holmes said there will be regression but it will be less and less.

Mike Cocoris** and Pastor Murphy of Amarillo Bible Church came to see us. There have been a few other area pastors and church people come in and offer assistance and comfort even though they don't know us.

Mary Bell went to hospital with me and Bob told her how much he appreciates her taking me in and asked, "What do you think of my baby?" He also asked if his girls could come see him. Asked who was teaching his classes and if he was getting paid. I said yes and he was so relieved and so grateful. When I tell of people writing, praying or calling he says many times, "They are precious; they mean so much to me."

I found comfort in verses Dr. Jackson gave me, "There hath no temptation taken you but such as is common to man: but God is faithful, who will not suffer you to be tempted above that ye are able; but will with the temptation also make a way to escape, that ye may be able to bear it" (1 Cor. 10:13) and "Blessed be God . . . the God of all comfort; Who comforteth us in all our tribulation, that we may be able to comfort them which are in any

38

trouble, by the comfort wherewith we ourselves are comforted of God" (2 Cor. 1:3,4).

Bob asks for his glasses now for first time.

I worry about his right eye as it doesn't work the same as the left one. It looks different and eyelid doesn't close.

The rash from penicillin reaction is so bad—itchy and red all over his body. Counter medicine is now being given.

He asked if plane crash was going home Sunday night or Sunday morning. He doesn't remember preaching Sunday a.m. He said, "It's all mixed up."

Even though he was so bad yesterday, he remembered I told him the John E. Mitchell Company of Dallas had sent flowers.

Had to go out in hail storm to go home in evening.

Wednesday, October 16

Natalie is three months old today. Through all this she has kept on a good schedule and remains her happy contented self. She's from the Lord and is a help to me—gets my mind off my anxiety and Bob's suffering.

When I got to the hospital, Bob was calling "nurse." It bothers me I can't be there and no one is with him when he needs help. But I know a nurse can't be there all the time. I shudder to think of him alone that first night out of ICU—one nurse told me they finally strapped him down; I think he also was given oxygen because the tank was there the next morning.

Dr. Hands had been in earlier and said Bob can go to Dallas Friday.

I called Dr. Muck** of FBHM—talked to his son David. Dr. Muck has been so concerned because Bob had been on a mission for him.

Called Dr. Prewitt about Bob's glasses and about his plane ticket which I can't find. I *painfully* went all through his clothes and wallet—clothes are covered with dried up blood! It's agony to look at them. I'll discard them as it bothers me to have them in my room. Dr. Prewitt advised me to go through carefully each section in his wallet and finally I found the ticket. Someone probably put it there from his coat pocket because I KNOW where he keeps things like that. Blood was all over it too. Dr. Prewitt said the briefcase was unlatched at crash; hope nothing was lost; brand new Bible has big crease in it. Dr. Holmes said they found his glasses all bent and also found a smashed pair which must have been Bob's.

Bob said Dr. Curtis came and tightened the wires in his jaws (suspension wires inside face) with tools and he screamed for pain and said it felt like his eye was popping out. He also got out of bed by himself to use the bathroom and fell and bruised his back severely. I feel bad I wasn't there to help.

Marie Keeler got me for supper and kept Natalie at night. Her car stalled and we had to sit in the car in the cold for 45 minutes and the baby cried. Her son-in-law came and then took me home.

Thursday, October 17

It's cold.

I didn't sleep much—heart heavy BUT GOD NEAR. I suppose I better take sleeping pill again tonight (thought I might not need them anymore).

Bob still doesn't know days or nights from mornings.

Barbara Hedger kept Natalie.

Mrs. Holmes went home from hospital; will be in wheelchair 5 weeks. Dr. Holmes will go home in 2 weeks but will be in wheelchair also.

It's so frustrating as I've tried to contact Dr. Hands to tell that Dr. Mabery is taking the case (Dr. Ryrie reminded me this should be done). I finally reached him; he said Bob can go Monday and it's my responsibility to make all arrangements. Oh, dear. Dr. Price said bleeding from the ear is the membrane over the skull and will clear up. Bob said it is roaring terribly in his ear.

Harold Bennett** and Dick Engle** called. Also Mother said so many calls come to Dallas and people are so worried and so kind and she is occupied with phone calls and visits of the kind neighbors. She was so impressed with one call from California when the fellow said, "The Lord can't let Dr. Lightner die; he's too valuable." Everyone is so nice all over the country; I don't know how they all got the news. Various churches where Bob has preached in the past (Elmira, Cincinnatus, DeRuyter, Rochester, Mt. Upton, Ross Corners and others) assure us of prayers and some even send money.

Dr. & Mrs. Graham from the Borger group came with substantial gift of money from the folks there to help with expenses. We are simply stunned! Dr. Graham also talked with me some more about the crash and possible causes, etc.

All day Bob seemed so tired and in forenoon just wasn't himself at all. He hadn't slept well. At night he was more like himself, worried about me and asks about the bills, where his wallet and money are, and more about the crash. But he didn't ask again if any were killed.

I called Mother. She said Harold, Ken and his mother back home are wondering and wondering about Bob's condition now. I feel bad that I can't find time to do the phoning I should—there are so many things to do here; I usually only get to bed near midnight till I care for everything.

Friday, October 18

Bob wanted to talk a lot. I spent the morning reading mail to him. I have packs of it and it keeps coming.

He questions me all the time about things and specifics. He has to close his eyes a lot because the right one quivers and hurts.

He remembers some things about Saturday night before the crash and Sunday morning leaving home, going to Love Field, parking the car and getting on Braniff. After that, he's blank.

He frets about me in traffic, etc. so I know he's getting better. When he sleeps, other parts of his body twitch. He told me he looked in the mirror and is satisfied with the way doctors fixed him, but he can sense Dr. Hale isn't satisfied. I think his nose has sunk in since the packing was taken out.

Dr. Hale came in and when he was finished looking at Bob, I followed him to the hall. I told him he's done a good job on the nose and asked if he is satisfied and he answered, "Of course, I'm never satisfied." I told him I was wondering if anything more could be done; if there is and they wanted to do more work, in light of Bob's life ahead and his type of work, I'm sure he could put up with a few days of discomfort—especially after all he's been through now. He said he was glad to hear that and they've been talking about it.

Bob's mouth and tongue are so sore, full of sores and raw from all the wires and hooks and surgery too. He doesn't drink very much as some of the juices burn. His rash is still bad and his back sore from the fall. One thing after the other, but he doesn't complain.

He has two slits on his upper lip that will show.

Kathryn picked me up in the morning and kept Natalie while I was at the hospital. Her husband, Alden, went to the airport and took care of getting tickets for our flight to Dallas Monday at 3:45. Airlines will let me go first class on my excursion ticket at no extra charge! I enjoyed visiting with Kathryn and her family—felt like I was with Karolyn. I was able to do my hair and also much phoning, arranging for ambulance on Monday, etc. They (the Whites) took Natalie to their church at night—couldn't get away afterwards they said, as people fussed over her.

42

Also talked to Dr. Mabery in Dallas. He'll make arrangements there for ambulance and for Bob to go to Presbyterian Hospital. He was so kind and understanding. He said he wants to get Bob well and then talk about any possible further surgery to fix the nose. I felt relieved.

Also called Pastor Rowland** in Johnson City, N.Y. and talked at length. I know the people there have been so concerned so gave him details.

Ken (Dr. Johnston) stops to see Bob regularly with encouraging words and Bob thinks so much of him for this concern. I've appreciated these days with the Johnstons and getting to know the family. Mary Bell and I have had many heart-to-heart talks too. I see how a doctor's family must be willing to have the daddy home for a brief time and then called out again and at any hour of day or night and maybe smash long awaited plans. They are dedicated to their work and the people they serve. The Johnstons have become attached to our baby and have taken good care of her and me, and tell me they'll miss us when we leave.

Saturday, October 19

Mary Bell had things to do so Marie Keeler got me for the day. Marie really has been wonderful through all this. She took me to store to get Bob robe and slippers as Dr. Hands said he can be up for a few steps. He's so weak.

I talked to Dr. Holmes at length. He tried to explain to me what he thinks happened. They were up the first time about 400 feet. Dr. Little was turning the switch that controls the airspeed and had some difficulty (this is the trim tab). Dr. Holmes told him to land the plane and take care of it—check it out. He thinks a big plane took off a few minutes before they did on their second takeoff. The cross winds and the vortex which is like a small tornado wind caused air turbulence and they were only up about 150 feet which was not high enough to bring the plane out of it or to glide a landing.

I talked to Dr. Hendricks and gave him information on our flight back to Dallas.

They took more X-rays of Bob's head.

In the afternoon they put Bob on a wheelchair to go see Dr. Holmes down the hall. He told Bob that Dr. Little was killed. This is first he knew it. Bob had told me earlier that all this has done one thing for him—took away desire to fly his own plane. Bob said he was not blaming anyone for the crash.

Spent most of the day reading mail. He gets tired and falls asleep easily.

Again he asked all the details, what girls did and how they took it when I told them he might die. He asks about our sisters and brothers—what they think.

He forgets what I told him a day or two before. He said all through these days he was all mixed up and wondered where he was and why here. I don't really know when he first recognized me. Before Tuesday he'd call me by name and seemed normal but didn't seem like "my Bob." After that though he started becoming himself.

When he got awake from one of his naps, he had been dreaming of eating a steak dinner. He is anxious to take the family out to eat. Bless his heart! And he'll be on liquids 6 weeks and it's so hard to get it too. But he's so cooperative with the nurses and doctors. They all seem to like him.

He still has air coming out of the hole in his throat when he talks or breathes. He seems anxious to see people, and is anxious to get home to Dallas.

He still says odd things. Things are confusing to him and he gets jumbled. For example, he asked about his tie and at the same time said, "You know, the cord to the shaver." (I never found his tie, guess it was discarded as were his glasses).

He sits up now in bed but says talking is so hard. And his eye bothers him too. I definitely think he does look different, but is real good.

At noon I called Bob's mother and explained how busy and running I am in strange city, 5 different homes and driving 3 or 4 different cars and taking care of arrangements and details and trying to be with Bob that I haven't called like I should. She was relieved to get news he is much better and she said Ken had called down here to the doctors to find out about his condition. Also she, Ken and Janet (his wife) are flying down next weekend.

Sunday, October 20

Called Bob on the phone in the morning and he answered it! Isn't that wonderful! He said he slept well; I did too. He's bothered that he can't hear out of his right ear and it roars.

Dr. Curtis was at the hospital when I got there. He had to do more tightening and shifting of the wires in Bob's jaws. Bob surely dreaded it as he talks a lot about the agony of the other time. I left the room but then he said afterwards it wasn't as bad as the other time. Dr. Curtis is trying his best with his tools to line up the jaws properly and to match the bite and to have teeth in middle. It's all so difficult because of many changes and shifting of features of his face and mouth. He came in three times to work at it. He really has done a good job as have the other surgeons in surgeries and care. Bob mentions often that they come in all the time and keep checking on him.

Johnstons took Natalie to church with them; people are so surprised to learn she is Lightner baby whose daddy was in plane crash they heard about. Went out to eat with Johnstons.

Got calls from Dan Gelatt (he says he'd like to fly down sometime to see Bob) and Dr. & Mrs. Jackson.

45

Dr. Prewitt came from Borger. He told Bob he was moving his arms and legs to get out of the plane after it crashed. It took the ambulance 28 minutes to get from the Borger hospital to Amarillo (50 miles) and Bob was "trying to get out" all the way. They told us the bleeding was very bad. And they had gasoline over them when the plane stopped cartwheeling.

Bob said while I was gone, Mr. Diebler* (he preached at Borger today) was in to see him. Other friends from Borger came too and also people from Amarillo Bible Church.

Doctors told Bob he has bad punctured eardrum (this is why he can't hear) and it's important he doesn't get water in it or it may get infected! He must keep cotton in. Drainage seems to be clearing up.

I went to Marie Keeler's again in the evening. She, Pat, Barbara and John (her daughters and son) came to see Bob.

I talked to Mother and girls (they asked if Natalie still has her hair; they're anxious for us to come home).

Bob is anxious to see the girls.

If you think you have problems, just look around at a hospital. Spending hours in ICU waiting room we all got acquainted with each others' cases and progress. Mrs. Rush's husband had a stroke, didn't recover—passed away. Yet, she was such a comfort to me and offered help. Mrs. McDugan's 25 year old husband also had a stroke and was not responding at all to therapy—future very dark—and they have small children. Yet, these ladies were so happy for me—I was able to take my husband home! I bow in humility and thanksgiving to the Lord that He chose to work so many miracles for us. May He receive the praise!

Monday, October 21

Dr. Hands said all records are duplicated and ready for me to take to Dallas. Business office again checked airport for possible insurance—there is none. We had to sign that if

46

Bob's Seminary hospitalization doesn't pay, we will. The amount is so vast that *we* can't pay—BUT GOD!

In morning I got the records in a folder, then went home to feed Natalie. Mary Bell and I went to meet the ambulance which was 15 minutes late. I was anxious and nervous. They used a lift to get Bob up in the plane. He says he has misgivings about flying. Natalie is having bowel trouble and is fussing. I didn't let on to Bob of the problem—thankful she slept on flight. Perhaps she senses my anxiety of this whole responsibility. It was good to have Mike Cocoris traveling on the same plane in case I needed help.

The flight was rough in spots! I read the detailed medical records. WHAT A MIRACLE GOD HAS WROUGHT!

Dr. Robinson* met Mike at Love Field. There was excitement as no ambulance was there to take Bob and airline officials seemed upset too. We didn't know plans had been changed and he was to be taken by car. Bob walked with help from the plane and then Dr. Robinson wheeled him for the long walk and then took us to the hospital. Mother and Elaine Getz met us and took the baby home and I went with Bob to admit him. Marie Harris** waited 1½ hrs. at emergency thinking he'd be brought there. She wants to be his private nurse for a few days! She took me home at night. The baby has been crying a lot. I felt keyed up and a wreck emotionally from all the responsibilities and excitement of the day—and also to think of the future, the long convalescence. I know the Lord would have me face each step one at a time, but can I do this?

Bob called the girls on the phone and Nancy cried to him. He cried some too. He wants to come home so bad.

I tried to do some paper work but can't concentrate.

Tuesday, October 22

11:00—Mother and I went to the hospital (a neighbor kept Natalie).

Mother couldn't decide whether to go back to Pennsylvania tomorrow or wait till Sunday. I really felt I needed her but hated to say, but she decided she'd wait till Sunday and go back with Ken and Janet, who are coming with Bob's mother on Saturday (his mother will stay 2 weeks and then Harold and Jane will come for a few days and she'll fly back with them).

Bob is thrilled with his doctors. They are fine Christians. He had extensive X-rays again. Doctors think he *must* have double vision, but he doesn't. He called at night and said he doesn't think he will be there long. He was moved from private to semi-private room now.

The Ryries, Walvoords and Hendricks visited him in evening.

At night Mother and I took the girls to Big Town for things they needed. Natalie seems to be getting better.

Wednesday, October 23

I was shocked when Marie Harris called in the morning and said Bob is being dismissed. She brought him home and gave extensive directions for his medications and care. He gets up and walks around but can't be up too long. He sleeps a lot. He is so glad to be home. Girls were surprised and were so good, didn't talk too much and excite him. We spent time at night reading mail. We are so touched with the kindnesses of everyone. The Scripture verses, tracts, poems they include are a blessing.

Bob is worried about his eye. He's trying hard to make it function like the other one.

It's good Mother decided to stay till Sunday. I couldn't have managed without her, since Nadine was sick this first night and I was also awake and up a lot with Bob. All his food must be liquid. I'm edgy and worried as must watch for fever—signs of infection which could result in meningitis. I also have wire cutters to cut the wires in case he'd get nauseated and would have to open jaws.

48

Thank the Lord for the miracle he is home so soon.

This whole experience is teaching me many lessons. When things go along fine we feel self-sufficient. But we really aren't. He is in control of all things and is our strength. Also many things that seemed important before are insignificant. The important thing we remember right now is that the Lord allowed us to have our daddy and we are together as a family. Also, we must not look ahead and worry about the many problems: how we'll get through further surgery, endless doctors' visits, caring for added responsibilities, and the financial needs of all of this. But I must go day by day and ask for *daily* strength. One of my beloved friends quoted these words in a letter to us:

"One day at a time, and the day is His day;
He hath numbered its hours, though they haste or delay.
His grace is sufficient; we walk not alone;
As the day, so the strength that He giveth His own."

—Annie Flint

And last, I have been negligent in personal witnessing. May I always be ready to speak a word for my Saviour and witness of His goodness and miracles wrought in our lives!

6

A MIRACLE of GRACE

"It was a miracle of course that three of the four of us survived the crash and that we did not have a fire because of the gasoline spillage. Another miracle was the fact that I survived fatty embolism, which has a very high mortality rate. Another miracle was the switches were off. I did not turn them off for I could not reach them, and Bille does not remember doing anything to them." In a personal letter to me Dr. Holmes wrote the above which expresses the sentiment of all the survivors.

The superintending care of God was manifested many times and in many ways through the tragedy God permitted. Though the specific purpose or purposes which He designed for this crash may never be known, everyone involved is a firm believer that God never makes a mistake. Surely God did not allow the crash without purpose. In truth, there are no accidents with Him. Our responsibility as His children is to submit ourselves to Him and His purposeful ways. Christians are not called upon to know why, but simply to trust God and rest in His loving care for His own.

Like Job-of-old the question, "Why do the righteous suffer?" often plagues the believer for an answer. We think we know why the unrighteous suffer but can't understand the hardships of the righteous. The answer is not always easy to give. Often it is impossible. Sometimes human suffering and trial are the result of sin. Through hardship, God often seeks to discipline us and woo us back to Himself. Inventory of our lives is always good to be sure that our sin has not been the cause of our suffering. Not all human suffering is the result of sin, however. Jesus Christ, the sinless Son of God suffered and died.

When asked who had sinned, the blind man or his parents, that he had been born blind, Jesus answered, "Neither . . . but that the works of God should be made manifest in him" (John 9:3).

Nowhere in the Bible is the Christian promised a flower-strewn pathway through life. The Scriptures abound with promise and evidence of trials and hardships for the children of God. Through them, God teaches us many things as He reveals His grace under times of testing. The child of God is promised the Saviour's presence through the deep waters. He said, "I will never leave thee, nor forsake thee" (Heb. 13:5).

So often we forget what Job forgot. He failed to realize that God had a perfect right to allow a righteous man to suffer. He works in mysterious ways His wonders to perform. To question the will and ways of God borders on blasphemy. In truth, it is an attempt to usurp His role as the sovereign Lord. Job complained often. He is not an example of one who was patient with his accusers either. Through all his unspeakable hardships and all the harrassment of his "friends," he never accused God. In this, his example should be followed. It is God's will that whatever befalls us, we trust in His infinite wisdom and rest in His protective grace.

After returning to my home in Dallas, among the many, many cards and letters from interested friends came one from my good friend, Dr. Robert T. Ketcham. Along with his words of greeting he mailed a plaque with these words on it: "Our Heavenly Father is too good to be unkind and too wise to make mistakes." What a help and comfort those words have been. They helped me to triumph through tragedy. I had heard Dr. Ketcham stress those very words from the pulpit. But now they somehow meant much more to me. During a time of real testing God gave those words to Dr. Ketcham and he has shared them with many since then.

God taught me and my family many things through this experience. How thankful I am for a wife, who through all the shock, stress and strain of those dreadful days remained her sweet, selfless, loving, and considerate self. What would *I* have done? and how would I have reacted if I had received the call that she was in critical condition and liable to die at any moment? Those questions have come to me many times since. On the Sunday night of October 6 when she received the news of my critical condition, she had to tell our two oldest daughters at once. The Lord wonderfully sustained and undergirded her and them. The grief, shock, fear, and responsibilities were overwhelming. The Lord marvelously upheld her moment by moment. He used many individuals who were willing to be used to accomplish His purposes. The fact that He uses people to accomplish His sovereign purposes has been reaffirmed to us.

From the time of the crash to the end of my period of recovery, there were many hurdles, new experiences, and adjustments to face. If all of them would have been known to us at one time or ahead of time, we would have fainted beneath the load. God, in His infinite wisdom, led us one step at a time. He gave grace commensurate with the need. The whole experience taught us patience and what it really means to walk with Him moment by moment. We could only cross bridges when we got to them. God's abundant grace was sufficient for every need. He is faithful!

During those days, and since, my wife and I have thought how terrible it would be to go through such an experience without the Lord. We would have had no place to turn in those trying hours if we had not been rightly related to God the Father through personal faith in God the Son. Without divine help, even the kind assistance of family and friends would have been inadequate to carry us through those deep waters.

Since we knew the Lord, the many friends who assisted us in so many ways during our need became channels of blessing to us and instruments in the Lord's hands to fulfill His purpose in our lives. The willingness and kindness of my mother and mother-in-law to come and help and my brothers Harold and Kenneth and their wives to visit us all the way from Pennsylvania was a tremendous source of blessing. Of course, not every member of our families could come to help, but all prayed.

In less than a month from the time of his injury Dr. Holmes was able to return to his medical profession in a wheelchair. On November 18 he drove his own car to the hospital and delivered a baby born to one of his patients. This was an unusually fast recovery for one who suffered fractures of the first and second lumbar vertebra and a fractured pelvis.

Mrs. Holmes also suffered severe injuries. She had a fractured heel, fractured ribs, and a fractured sixth thoracic vertebra. Added to these were a concussion, multiple bruises and lacerations of the face and head and a fracture of the left radius (arm). For reasons known only to God complete healing and recovery did not come to Mrs. Holmes as soon as was expected. A bone graft was necessary on her left forearm. This involved the necessity of a cast for a prolonged period of time. The Lord gave her patience and courage as healing came.

The family and friends of Dr. Little suffered a tremendous loss. There are few men in the medical profession who are dedicated believers in Jesus Christ. Dr. Little was such a man. God saw fit to take him home and we dare not question why. How wonderful to know that God has not left Himself without a witness. Dr. James Bolton, brother of Dr. Jack Bolton, my oral surgeon in Dallas, has taken over Dr. Little's dental practice in Borger. He too is a born-again man and desires to serve Christ.

The days of convalescence were days of real blessing to me. In addition to the hundreds of cards and letters from interested friends, many others were used of God to meet our needs. The group insurance which the Seminary makes available was in force for me just five days before the crash. That was another token of God's grace. Many individuals brought in food and helped in other ways during those days when help was needed most. Churches, student bodies, and individuals prayed and assisted us financially. These prayers God answered and the gifts made it possible for us to pay the percentage of the cost not covered by the insurance.

It has been a genuine challenge to be chosen of God to be used by Him to bring blessing and spiritual enrichment to so many others. Why He has done this I do not know, but we do believe it was divinely ordered. We have had opportunities to testify of God's grace to many for a long time after the crash and recovery. Wherever we went and to whomever we talked, it was a natural thing to talk about the miracle of grace.

While my wife was waiting in the waiting room for me to come out of the December 12 surgery, she had occasion to talk to a grief-stricken woman about the Lord. When she wrote to doctors expressing gratitude for their untiring efforts on my behalf, she also testified of our trust in the Lord. People usually call my experience "good luck." They often say, "You were lucky." Not so! This was all the result of God's marvelous grace in our lives. The impact for good which this experience has had upon me, my family, and friends cannot be measured. Eternity alone will reveal its accomplishments for the glory of God.

"Near catastrophic" was the way Dr. Hands of Amarillo described my physical condition immediately after the crash. He wrote these words on the medical report he mailed to the insurance company. With a compound skull fracture, right eye blowout and broken floor, broken and smashed nose, upper lip cut through and through and the cut extending up into the nose and out at midnose, floating maxilla, broken jaw, multiple broken facial bones, crushed right wrist and dislocated thumb, cuts and bruises on arms and body, and all the potential hazards these injuries involved, it is little wonder he termed my condition "near catastrophic."

The concerned interest of the six medical specialists who treated me there in Amarillo was genuine and intense. They were Dr. Sebel Hands, general surgeon and in charge; Dr. Stephen Curtis, oral surgeon; Dr. William Hale, eye, ear, nose, and throat specialist; Dr. William Price, neurosurgeon; Dr. Robert Hyde, orthopedist; and Dr. Richard Archer, internist. They did not know me and it would not have made any difference if they had known who I was. Their concern was not what political or religious views I held. Neither did they ask whether they would get paid for their emergency services. They didn't even quibble with each other over their differences and past achievements. The paramount concern of each one of them at the crucial moment was my physical well being. With this uppermost in their minds they dedicated themselves to the task with relentless efforts.

From this, the believer in Jesus Christ should learn a lesson. In our service for Him many things are important, but one thing matters and it matters most. That one thing is our fellowship with the Lord. When that is healthy, we will arise to the need of giving ourselves wholly to His service without fear or favor of other people.

My doctors often expressed surprise and amazement at my swift and unusual recovery. Even before I was fully conscious, they told Dr. Hendricks, who kept checking on my condition, things like this: "We can't explain it," "We never saw that before," "We don't understand it." The four doctors who attended me when I came from Amarillo to Dallas expressed similar words. Each one of these men is not only a specialist in his field but also a dedicated Christian. Dr. Trevor Mabery, otolaryngologist; Dr. Jack Bolton, oral surgeon; Dr. Jack Cooper, ophthalmologist; and Dr. George Sibley, orthopedist, are all active in their local churches. They rejoiced with me as God answered the prayers of thousands of friends all over the nation and even in some foreign countries. We received 350 letters and cards with notes attached, expressing interest and assuring us of prayer for my condition and for the family. In some cases entire church families and student bodies of Christian schools held us before the throne of grace.

Dr. Mabery's examination of me revealed the need for further surgery on my nose and skin graft surgery on my right eardrum which had a very large hole in it because of the head injuries. Long before the nose surgery was scheduled, I began to return to more and more of my normal duties. Very early in November, I was driving my car. Even before the cast and stitches were removed from my right arm and thumb, I was engaged in a writing ministry. Some time before the October 6 tumble of the Tri-Pacer I had committed myself to writing thirteen adult Sunday school lessons on the Book of James. Only four of the lessons were finished when the crash occurred. Since the due date deadline was nearing, I proceeded to write these as soon as possible. X-rays taken on November 4 showed that my wrist had knitted beautifully and Dr. Sibley was pleased with the results.

The burden to stand before the Dallas Theological Seminary student body and give testimony to God's grace grew heavy upon my heart. It was decided that November 6, the scheduled day of prayer, would be the best time for it. I will never forget the surprised and amazed look on the eyes of those men as they saw me walk on the platform and heard me give a few words of testimony. How fitting for the day of prayer! I was a living answer to their prayers. They, along with the faculty, had prayed much. They had given sacrifically too. There were moist eyes all over the Chafer chapel that day. God was praised for His marvelous grace.

On November 21 Dr. Bolton clipped the wires which had held my jaws together very tightly. These wires had been on for about seven weeks, and all that time my mouth felt as though I was biting as hard as I could. During that time I was on a completely liquid diet. All my food was received through a straw. Many times I would think and dream of the privilege of chewing solids. A piece of butter bread never tasted so good as when those wires were cut. Though it was painful to move my jaws again and though the braces and hooks still on my teeth gouged my mouth, it was a thrill simply to chew food.

On December 2 Dr. Cooper gave me a thorough eye examination. All the doctors feared that my right eye would drop because of the severe and crushing wounds received in the bone structure just beneath it. This would have caused double vision. Dr. Cooper gave me the excellent report, however, that my eyes were perfectly normal and the facial paralysis, which had continued for weeks after the crash, was gone! He also added that there was no medical explanation for this. There was a marked improvement over what he had seen in his first visit to my room in the Dallas hospital when I had just been transferred from Amarillo.

Drs. Mabery and Bolton scheduled my Dallas surgery for December 12 at 7:30 a.m. Dr. Bolton was to remove the thin suspension or traction wires which were attached to small holes drilled in the bones above my eyes, extending down inside the face and connected to the upper jaw braces. These had been installed to keep the facial bones and jaws held tightly in proper place so they would knit and heal. Also he was to remove the metal braces which were attached to the upper and lower teeth. All this equipment had been placed in my face and mouth by Dr. Curtis, oral surgeon, in Amarillo. In surgery when Dr. Bolton discovered that the wires had embedded so deeply in the eye bones that he could not pull them out through the mouth, he had to make small incisions above my eyes to enable him to remove the wires. Dr. Bolton confessed amazement at the way my jawbone knitted so well and so fast.

57

The most important part of this surgery was a nasal-septal reconstruction and rhino plasty performed by Dr. Mabery. The operation involved removing the bony hump on the right side, grafting tissue at the place where it was destroyed, and straightening the S shaped cartilage so that air could pass through the right nostril. The work of both surgeons took 3½ hours. Afterwards Dr. Mabery expressed amazement at the way the surgery went and the results of it. Normally, one who had such severe injuries would need to have more than one operation to correct the problem. As far as these men were concerned, they were working on a living miracle. And that they were! The healing and recovery from this surgery were fantastically rapid. No expected fever developed and no pain pills were even required.

.On one occasion, in his office after the surgery, Dr. Mabery again checked my right eardrum. A puzzled look came over his face after he had been looking in my ear for some time. He then looked in my ear with a microscope and studied it intently. What he saw caused him and me to rejoice. The large hole in the punctured eardrum had healed itself shut except for a hole the size of a pin. This was another miracle! Dr. Mabery said it was cause for rejoicing. Holes the size he had seen in my ear simply do not close by themselves, especially not in adults. His first look in my ear when I came from Amarillo told him immediately that skin graft was an absolute necessity. When he first told me that, I began to pray that another surgery would not be necessary. God answered prayer again! Though there is an impairment of hearing in the right ear, it does not require surgery.

Around the first part of January, I was feeling so well physically that I thought about going back to Borger to preach. The group there still did not have a pastor. Men from Dallas Theological Seminary had been assisting them each week. I only mentioned this to my wife, not wanting to push myself on the folks. A day or two later I was in

Dr. Evans' office and he said, "Would you like to go to Borger again to preach?" What a challenge this presented to me! I had not preached since October 6, the morning of the crash. "Let me pray and think about it a few days," I said. My good wife and I talked and prayed about it. We decided that even though it would be hard on the family, I should take advantage of the opportunity. The connotations of flying to Borger to preach naturally aroused fears and anxiety for us all. But we realized it would be best to face it squarely and overcome apprehensions by committing it fully to the Lord. Reservations were made on Trans Texas Airways, now named Texas International, to fly from Dallas Love Field to Amarillo.

It was a genuine thrill to meet those dear friends again and to give the Lord the praise for all He had done. The text of Scripture in Romans 8:28-39 from which I preached that Sunday was more precious than ever to me. God had permitted me to go through experiences which taught me many things about all things working together for good to them who love God and are the called according to His purpose. The faith of those dear people was strengthened tremendously. They had prayed earnestly and given sacrificially and now the answer to their prayers stood before them. I could almost see faith in their eyes.

In the afternoon several of us went to the site of the crash which at that time could be located readily because of the holes and torn-up macadam. I met the men who rescued us from that twisted wreckage and was able to give God praise. It was all a miracle of God's grace.

Tuesday, January 21, 1969 I was able to return to the classroom and my teaching responsibilities at Dallas Theological Seminary. This was a great thrill to again be engaged in the work to which God had called me.

The words that still come to mind as I often think back upon it all are, "Great things He hath done." This is abundantly true, even in times of tragedy.

7

COMFORT for SUFFERING SAINTS

The following represents a selection of some of the passages of Scripture which proved to be such a help to us during the days of suffering and convalescence. Many of these were given to us by concerned friends. Quotations are from the King James Version.

"My soul, wait thou only upon God; for my expectation is from him" (Ps. 62:5).

"My flesh and my heart faileth: but God is the strength of my heart, and my portion for ever" (Ps. 73:26).

"For the LORD God is a sun and shield: the LORD will give grace and glory: no good thing will he withhold from them that walk uprightly" (Ps. 84:11).

"He that dwelleth in the secret place of the most High shall abide under the shadow of the Almighty" (Ps. 91:1).

"And say unto him, Take heed, and be quiet; fear not, neither be fainthearted . . ." (Isa. 7:4).

"Fear thou not; for I am with thee: be not dismayed; for I am thy God: I will strengthen thee; yea, I will help thee; yea, I will uphold thee with the right hand of my righteousness" (Isa. 41:10).

"It is of the LORD'S mercies that we are not consumed, because his compassions fail not. They are new every morning: great is thy faithfulness" (Lam. 3:22,23).

"The LORD is good, a strong hold in the day of trouble; and he knoweth them that trust in him" (Nahum 1:7).

"And we know that all things work together for good to them that love God, to them who are the called according to his purpose" (Rom. 8:28).

"There hath no temptation taken you but such as is common to man: but God is faithful, who will not suffer you to be tempted above that ye are able; but will with the temptation also make a way to escape, that ye may be able to bear it" (1 Cor. 10:13).

"Grace be to you and peace from God our Father, and from the Lord Jesus Christ. Blessed be God, even the Father of our Lord Jesus Christ, the Father of mercies, and the God of all comfort; Who comforteth us in all our tribulation, that we may be able to comfort them which are in any trouble, by the comfort wherewith we ourselves are comforted of God" (2 Cor. 1:2-4).

"Humble yourselves therefore under the mighty hand of God, that he may exalt you in due time: Casting all your care upon him; for he careth for you" (1 Pet. 5:6,7).

Among the many choice poems and sayings which were given to us here is a sampling. It is hoped that these may be used of God to help others in the hour of need.

I Needed the Quiet

I needed the quiet so He drew me aside.
Into the shadows where we could confide.
Away from the bustle where all the day long
I hurried and worried when active and strong.

I needed the quiet tho at first I rebelled
but gently, so gently, my cross He upheld
And whispered so sweetly of spiritual things
Tho weakened in body, my spirit took wings
To heights never dreamed of when active and gay.
He loved me so greatly He drew me away.

I needed the quiet. No prison my bed,
But a beautiful valley of blessings instead—
A place to grow richer in Jesus to hide.
I needed the quiet so He drew me aside.

—Alice Hansche Mortenson

Though everything without fall into confusion,
and though thy body be in pain and suffering,
and thy soul in desolation and distress,
yet let thy spirit be unmoved by it all,
placid and serene, delighted in and with its
God inwardly, and with His good pleasure outwardly.

—Gerhard Tersteegen

God Knows Best

Our Father knows what's best for us,
So why should we complain—

We always want the sunshine,
But He knows there must be rain—

We love the sound of laughter
And the merriment of cheer,
But our hearts would lose their tenderness
If we never shed a tear . . .

Our Father tests us often
With suffering and with sorrow,
He tests us, not to punish us,
But to help us meet tomorrow . . .

For growing trees are strengthened
When they withstand the storm,
And the sharp cut of the chisel
Gives the marble grace and form . . .

God never hurts us needlessly,
And He never wastes our pain
For every loss He sends to us
Is followed by rich gain . . .

And when we count the blessings
That God has so freely sent,
We will find no cause for murmuring
And no time to lament . . .

For our Father loves His children,
And to Him all things are plain,
So He never sends us *pleasure*
When the *soul's deep need is pain* . . .

So whenever we are troubled,
And when everything goes wrong,
It is just God working in us
To make our *spirit strong*.

—Helen Steiner Rice

63

Great Faith That Smiles
Is Born of Great Trials

It's easy to say, *"In God we trust"*
When life is radiant and fair,
But the test of faith is only found
When there are burdens to bear—
For our claim to faith in the "sunshine"
Is really *no faith at all*
For when roads are smooth and days are bright
Our need for God is so small,
And no one discovers the fullness
Or the greatness of God's love
Unless he has walked in the "darkness"
With only a *light* from *Above*—
For the faith to endure whatever comes
Is born of sorrow and trials,
And strengthened only by discipline
And nurtured by self-denials—
So be not disheartened by troubles,
For trials are the "building blocks"
On which to erect a *fortress* of *faith*
Secure on God's "ageless rocks."

—Helen Steiner Rice

The Haven of His Love

The Sea of Life is rough and stormy,
And my craft is small and frail;
But with God's hand upon the wheel,
I can weather any gale!

And when doubts and fears assail me
And seek to overwhelm—

In perfect peace I rest securely
For God is at the helm!

—Jon Gilbert

The Weaver

My life is but a weaving
Between my Lord and me,
I cannot choose the colors
He worketh steadily.

Ofttimes He weaveth sorrow,
And I in foolish pride
Forget He sees the upper
And I, the under side.

Nor till the loom is silent
And the shuttles cease to fly
Shall God unroll the canvas
And explain the reason why.

The dark threads are as needful
in the Weaver's skillful hand
As the threads of gold and silver
In the pattern He has planned.

—Author unknown

Windows

When hardships come to my life
May they not appall;
May I not consider burdens as
An insurmountable wall.

May I not let earthly trials
Fill my heart and mind with fear:

May I never cease to trust in God,
Though unpleasant things appear.

And if I sin or lose my way,
May I not be in despair;
If roads are hard and pathway steep,
May I never cease to dare.

May troubles not be like blank walls
Through which light can find no place;
But rather shining windows be,
Through which I can see God's face.

And see just Him when testings come,
Praying, "Father, keep me true,
Teach me to see in every trial
What You would have me do.

"Give me faith, though I can't understand
Why all these troubles are mine;
Teach me to count them as from Thee,
And say, 'Not my will, but Thine.'"

—Ruby Lydia Lamb

One Day at a Time

One day at a time, and the day is His day;
He hath numbered its hours, though they haste or delay
His grace is sufficient; we walk not alone;
As the day, so the strength that He giveth His own.

—Annie Johnson Flint

He Was There

Jesus heard when you prayed last night,
He talked with God about you;

Jesus was there when you fought that fight,
He is going to bring you through.

Jesus knew when you shed those tears,
But you did not weep alone;
For the burden you thought too heavy to bear,
He made His very own.

Jesus Himself was touched by that trial,
Which you could not understand;
Jesus stood by as you almost fell,
And lovingly grasped your hand.

Jesus cared when you bore that pain;
Indeed, He bore it too;
He felt each pang, each ache in your heart,
Because of His love for you.

Jesus was grieved when you doubted His love,
But He gave you grace to go on;
Jesus rejoiced as you trusted Him,
The only trustworthy One.

His Presence shall even be with you,
No need to be anxious or fret;
Wonderful Lord! He was there all the time,
He has never forsaken you yet.

—Nell Hawkins

Appendix

The following was written by Lyndsay Holmes, the daughter and one of four children of Bob and Bille Holmes, who were aboard the Tri-Pacer when it crashed. This testimony was written first as a theme for an English class in high school. Later it appeared in the local newspaper in Borger, Texas a short while after the crash and is reproduced here in full.

Now My Life's Bright!

"Hi! I surely did like the sing-in tonight. I heard you wrote all those songs yourself."

"Well, thank you, but no, I didn't really. You see, God wrote them for me."

This is how it all started, with just a simple conversation. This conversation grew to be the most important conversation that I've ever held in my lifetime. It was with this simple introduction, that Greg went on to tell me what God had done for him, and what He could do for me.

I was spellbound. I could tell he had the Something I knew was missing from my life. And, he was showing me how to find it.

He told me, "I often compare my life to that television commercial where the woman's wash is clean and white, but when she used Bold, it was bright. My life, before I found God, was clean and white, but now it's bright!"

How like my own life this seemed. It was comparatively clean and white, but nothing ever seemed to go just the way it should. Something always seemed to be going wrong. I was the kind of person who, when things went wrong, everyone would know it. It would be written all over my face.

But not so with Greg. Even in the very short time that I had known him, I knew it was not that way with him. I found out later that this is a characteristic that Christians have, a light, a Christ-light shining in their eyes.

So, I decided this was the kind of life I wanted. I accepted Christ into my life that night, not only as my personal Savior, but also as the Lord of my life.

This was the turning point of my life. I read once that being a Christian must interfere with our way of living and make it better. This is so true in my case, and praise the Lord because of it.

Immediately, I began to see the more apparent gifts that God will give a Christian. I had heard at a talk the same week that I accepted Christ, that you can give God something, and He gives back to you often much more than you gave Him. So you give Him more, and He multiplies it again. This sounded pretty good, so, having no visible means of acquiring any money, I made a pledge on faith of twenty dollars to a nondenominational church camp. Not long after, I received a request to instruct a private swimming class, plus some offers for babysitting jobs. At the end of one month, I had earned over fifty dollars.

The Lord has also blessed me by giving me small problems to help build up my faith and strength so that I might face larger ones. He taught me that to get anywhere, I must rely on Him. When I was taking a swimming course for three hours a night, I would come home so tired and frustrated that I could not stand it. Then I realized that God was standing by, ready to help. All He needed from me were the words, "I give up. You take over now." So, I said this and then He started in. I ended up passing the course with flying colors, and a good disposition.

After having basic training such as this, God must have decided it was time for a bigger test. My parents were both hurt badly in a plane wreck. Our family was split up for three weeks and then my parents were both in wheelchairs for about the same length of time afterward. But, I had learned my lessons well. Even though at times I would forget, I would always come back to the fact that if I'd let God take control, everything would turn out okay. He took care of things beautifully once I gave up on it.

So, you see, when God showed me how to put that extra Something in my life that I had looked for so long, He also showed me the answer to all my problems, past, present, and future, large and small. Sure, I mess up a lot and still try to call the shots myself. But I know now that the only way to really live is with Christ.

"Now thanks be unto God, which always causeth us to triumph in Christ. . ." (2 Corinthians 2:14).